Paleo in 5

Quick & Easy 5 Minute Paleo & Gluten-Free Recipes for Super Busy People

Lucy Fast

Just to say Thank You for Purchasing this Book I want to give you a gift <u>100% absolutely FREE</u>

A Copy of My Upcoming Special Report
"Paleo Pantry: The Beginner's Guide to What Should and Should NOT be in Your Paleo Kitchen"

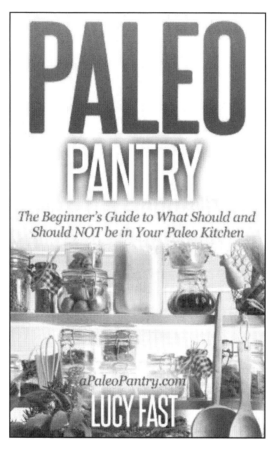

Go to <u>www.aPaleoPantry.com</u>
to Reserve Your FREE Copy

Table of Contents

Introduction

I want to thank you and congratulate you for purchasing *"Paleo in 5: Quick & Easy 5 Minute Paleo & Gluten-Free Recipes for Super Busy People"*. This book contains proven steps and strategies on how to cook gourmet Paleo meals in minutes.

Modern society is firmly entrenched in a culture of fast food with "convenience" being the primary order of the day.

Why?

Well because we are all busy, that's why. Life is HECTIC! Most families cannot manage on one income anymore and people are struggling to survive in such a fast paced modern world. And unfortunately the thing that suffers and gets sacrificed is cooking. Honestly, how many of us have time at the end of a long busy work day to make a healthy and nutritious meal for our families especially when supervising homework sessions or getting tired and cranky children bathed, fed and to bed?

Between work commitments, kids, and housework, it's sometimes a wonder that our families get fed at all, and if you do manage a home cooked meal, you certainly don't manage to cook one every night. For most people, fast food is a staple part of their diet, forming at least three, if not more meals on the menu every week.

This spells disaster if you are a Paleoite!

Traditional fast food is just not an option once you have made the lifestyle choice to go Paleo, so does that mean you are now bound to spend hours in the kitchen at the end of the day trying to whip up something beyond boiled chicken breasts and broccoli??

Absolutely and emphatically a loud resounding NO! I am pleased to tell you, that you can have Paleo fast food, probably in less time than you would wait in the queue at a fast food joint. Just imagine, steak to order, fresh vegetables cooked to perfection, delicious seafood and fish in next to no time.

What if I told you that you could prepare the healthiest food, packed full of flavor, stick to Paleo principles AND do it all in 5 minutes to boot? Well before you haul out the fire extinguisher to douse my flaming pants – hear me out!

Paleo is not a life sentence to bland food forever. If you truly embrace the lifestyle, it shall set you free! No more worry about aches, pains and ailments, no more worry about lifestyle diseases and sickness. Now I am not going to lecture you on the merits of Paleo, because if you are reading this book, you already are well-versed in what you should and shouldn't do/eat.

What I am offering you here is the tool to stick to your Paleo lifestyle, even on those manic days when you are rushed off your feet and find your car on auto pilot to Mickey D's (you all know what I'm talking about). On those days when you wonder if it's all worth it, or not just easier to quickly stop at the store and buy some microwave meals instead of preparing the chicken breasts you have defrosting on the kitchen counter at home – that's when you NEED this book!

I have chosen 36 awesome recipes that are absolutely indispensable – yes, I used the word "indispensable", because they will literally change your life. I have compiled a selection of dinner meals (because that's what we are all really after isn't it – quick, easy and healthy dinners) that can be cooked in minutes – yes folks, once you master the art of multi-tasking, you will churn these meals out in 5 minutes flat.

Pretty much all of the ingredients I have chosen can be picked up at the store already cut/sliced/chopped/julienned, so all you have to do is open a bag – easy huh?! For those of you that have a few extra minutes to spare you can chop them yourself if you prefer, but why, why, why, would you want to make work for yourself?

C'mon people, I'm giving you an out here! The trick to fast Paleo food is to know what to ask for. When buying meat, go for the thinner cuts that will cook quicker. If you don't want to pound the meat yourself, ask you butcher to do it for you, then all you need to do when you get home is unwrap it and throw it in the hot pan.

My chicken dishes can all be made with pre-cooked rotisserie chicken (or the rotisseries can be substituted for the chicken you would cook in each one), so the most effort you will have to make is a quick stop at the store on the way home. I have limited ingredients to a few for each recipe, as measuring, weighing etc… all take up precious time. Naturally these recipes are versatile enough that if you feel like something more adventurous over the weekend you can jazz them up to suit your tastes.

On days when you do find yourself with a bit of extra time, stock up on things like Paleo mayonnaise, stocks, broths, salsa's and sauces. That way you will never be left wanting (or tossing pots and pans across the kitchen) on busy days when you need to throw something together.

There is absolutely no good reason or excuse to ditch your Paleo lifestyle ever, so get reading. I hope these recipes will bring you as much delight as they did me.

Thanks again for purchasing this book, I hope you enjoy it!

Lucy Fast

Chop Chop Chicken!

Chicken with Mushroom Sauce
Yields: 4 Servings

Ingredients:

8 chicken thighs – skinless, boneless and pounded flat
1 lb. mushrooms – thinly sliced
1 cup organic or homemade chicken stock
½ cup parsley – finely chopped
1 onion – thinly sliced
6 tablespoons olive oil
4 tablespoons ghee
1 tablespoon garlic powder
Salt and pepper to taste

Method:
1. Preheat 2 non-stick pans over a medium high heat. Add 3 tablespoons of olive oil to each pan.
2. In the first pan add the chicken thighs and season them with the garlic powder.
3. Cook the chicken for 2 minutes per side.
4. In the second pan, add the onions and mushrooms and cook on high until the mushrooms begin to brown, then add the chicken stock. Cook for 1 minute and then stir in the ghee.
5. If the sauce is thick, simply thin it out with some water.
6. To serve, place the chicken onto a plate, top with the mushroom sauce and garnish with the chopped parsley.
7. Make your peace with seconds!

Greek-Style Chicken
Yields: 4 Servings

Ingredients:

8 chicken thighs – skinless, boneless and pounded flat
28 oz. can crushed tomatoes
1 cup olives – pitted
1 onion - chopped
4 garlic cloves - chopped
4 tablespoons olive oil
1 tablespoon rosemary
Salt and pepper to taste

Method:
1. Heat up two non-stick pans over a medium high heat and add 2 tablespoons of olive oil to each pan.
2. Season the chicken with the rosemary and add it to the first pan.
3. While the chicken browns, add the onions and garlic to the second pan and sauté on high for 2 minutes, then add the tomatoes and olives.
4. Allow the sauce to come to a gentle boil and then simmer for a minute.
5. Serve the chicken topped with the sauce.
6. It's divine!

Chicken Salad with Onion and Red Pepper
Yields: 2 Servings

Ingredients for the Salad:
4 cups salad greens
1 cup chicken – cooked and diced
1 red pepper – julienned
1 onion – thinly sliced
1 tablespoon freshly chopped parsley

Ingredients for the Mayonnaise:
2 egg yolks
¾ cup olive oil
1 garlic clove - chopped
1 tablespoon lemon juice
1 tablespoon vinegar

Method:
1. Add all the salad ingredients to a large bowl and toss to combine.
2. Place the egg yolks, ¼ cup olive oil, garlic, lemon juice and vinegar into a jug and blend using an immersion blender. When it is incorporated, slowly pour in the rest of the olive oil and keep blending until the mixture starts to thicken and resemble mayonnaise.
3. Pour the mayonnaise over the salad and toss well.
4. Serve immediately.
5. Delightful!

Super Easy Chicken Curry
Yields: 4 Servings

Ingredients:

1 whole pre-cooked rotisserie chicken – skin removed and shredded
2 cups coconut milk
¼ cup freshly chopped coriander
4 tablespoons green or red curry paste

Method:

1. Whisk the curry paste into the coconut milk.
2. Place the mixture into a saucepan and bring to the boil.
3. Add the chicken, reduce the heat to a simmer and allow the chicken to heat through.
4. Serve with freshly chopped coriander garnish.
5. Would you ever have thought you could have scrumptious curry in 5 minutes?

Chicken and Veggie Skewers
Yields: 4 Servings

Ingredients:

2 chicken breasts – skinless, boneless and cut into cubes
1 onion – cut into chunks
1 bell pepper – cut into chunks
2 zucchini – cut into chunks
8 cherry tomatoes
8 mushrooms
4 tablespoons olive oil
1 tablespoon rosemary
1 tablespoon thyme
Salt and pepper to taste

Method:
1. Fire up the Gas Grill! Or if you prefer to cook indoors – heat the broiler.
2. Arrange the chicken and vegetables on skewers, drizzle with olive oil and season with the rosemary, thyme, salt and pepper.
3. Place the skewers onto the BBQ or under the grill and cook for 2 ½ minutes each side.
4. Serve immediately and enjoy!

Curried Chicken Salad
Yields: 1 Serving

<u>*Ingredients:*</u>

2 cups mixed salad greens
½ cup precooked rotisserie chicken -- shredded or diced
¼ cup Paleo mayonnaise
¼ cup red onion – diced
¼ cup chopped apple
3 tablespoons chopped walnuts
1 tablespoon freshly chopped coriander
2 teaspoons curry powder

<u>*Method*</u>:
1. Mix the curry powder and mayonnaise together.
2. Place the rest of the ingredients into a big mixing bowl and toss to combine.
3. Stir through the curried mayonnaise dressing and toss well.
4. Serve immediately.
5. Absolutely amazing!

Turbo Turkey

Kitchen Sink Salad *(It's got everything BUT the Kitchen sink in it…)* **Yields: 1 Serving**

Ingredients:

¼ head of Romaine lettuce – torn into bite sized pieces
6 slices cucumber
2 slices deli turkey – roughly chopped
½ tomato – sliced
½ an avocado – peeled, pitted and cut into chunks
½ carrot - sliced
¼ red onion – thinly sliced
1 celery stalk – sliced
1 tablespoon olive oil
1 tablespoon balsamic vinegar
Salt and pepper to taste

Method:
1. Place all the salad ingredients into a bowl and toss lightly with the olive oil and balsamic.
2. Season with salt and pepper and serve immediately.
3. A deliciously light dinner perfect for those hot summers nights.

Fancy Fruity Turkey in a Flash
Yields: 4 Servings

<u>*Ingredients:*</u>

4 turkey cutlets
2 apples – cored and cut into wedges
1 cup cranberries
1 cup orange juice or water
Juice of 1 lemon
1 tablespoon olive oil

<u>*Method:*</u>
1. Heat the olive oil in a large non-stick pan over a medium high heat.
2. While the oil is heating up pound the turkey cutlets until they are about ½ an inch thick, then place them into the pan and cook until they are brown on both sides.
3. Remove the turkey from the pan and add the apples and cranberries and deglaze the pan with the orange juice or water.
4. Cook for about 2 minutes until the apples and cranberries start to soften, then remove from the heat.
5. Serve the turkey cutlets with the fruity dressing and finish off with a drizzle of lemon juice.
6. Superb!

Turkey with Spicy Sun-Dried Tomato Sauce
Yields: 4 Servings

Ingredients:

4 turkey cutlets – pounded to ½ inch thickness
2 cups mushrooms – thinly sliced
1 cup organic or homemade chicken stock
1 cup sun-dried tomatoes – sliced
¼ cup parsley – finely chopped
1 onion – thinly sliced
2 garlic cloves – chopped
6 tablespoons olive oil
4 tablespoon ghee
½ teaspoon cayenne pepper (or to taste)

Method:
1. Heat up two non-stick pans over a medium high heat and add 3 tablespoons of olive oil to each one.
2. Add the turkey cutlets to one pan and cook until browned – about 2 minutes per side.
3. While they cook, add the onions and mushrooms to the other pan and sauté on a high heat for 1 minute, then add the chicken stock and sun-dried tomatoes.
4. Cook for a further 2 minutes and then stir in the ghee.
5. Remove the sauce from the heat and stir through the parsley.
6. Serve the turkey with the sauce on top.
7. Scrumptious!

Turkey with Spicy Broccoli
Yields: 4 Servings

<u>*Ingredients:*</u>

4 turkey cutlets – pounded thin
4 cups broccoli florets
1 cup almond flour
½ cup water
2 eggs – beaten
4 garlic cloves - minced
6 tablespoons olive oil
1 tablespoon dried sage
2 teaspoons red pepper flakes

<u>*Method:*</u>

1. Heat up two non-stick pans over a medium high heat and add 3 tablespoons of olive oil to each.
2. Mix the almond flour and sage together in a bowl.
3. Beat the eggs together in another bowl, then dip the turkey cutlets into the eggs and then dredge them in the flour and sage mixture taking care to coat the meat on all sides.
4. Add them to one of the pans and cook for about 2 minutes per side.
5. In the second pan, add the broccoli, garlic and red pepper flakes and cook for 2 minutes, then add the water, cover and cook for a further 2 minutes until the broccoli is tender crisp.
6. Serve the turkey with a side of spicy broccoli for a deliciously healthy meal in minutes.
7. Enjoy!

Perfect Pork Pronto

Bacon Loaded Sweet Potato
Yields: 1 Serving

<u>*Ingredients:*</u>

1 sweet potato
2 bacon rashers
½ an avocado – peeled and sliced
½ tablespoon olive oil
½ tablespoon balsamic
Salt and pepper to taste

<u>*Method:*</u>
1. Prick the sweet potato with a fork a few times, place on a microwave safe plate and microwave for 4 minutes.
2. While the sweet potato cooks, heat up a non-stick pan and cook the bacon until it's crispy (about 2 minutes per side).
3. Slice the avocado.
4. When the sweet potato is cooked, slice it in half lengthways and top with the avocado slices.
5. Crumble the bacon over the top of the avocado and drizzle with balsamic vinegar and olive oil.
6. Season with salt and pepper and serve.
7. Incredibly delicious – enjoy!

Simple Sweet Pork Stir Fry
Yields: 4 – 6 Servings

<u>*Ingredients:*</u>

2 lb. pork fillet – sliced thinly
3 apples – cored and diced
1 onion - diced
1 cup apple juice – no added sugar
6 tablespoons olive oil
4 tablespoons ghee
1 tablespoon cinnamon

<u>*Method:*</u>
1. Heat two non-stick pans over a medium high heat and add 3 tablespoons of olive oil to each.
2. Add the onions and pork to the first pan and sauté until starting to brown.
3. Add the apples, cinnamon and apple juice to the second pan and allow to cook on high for 2 minutes until the apples begin to soften and then stir in the ghee.
4. Serve the pork topped with the apples and enjoy. YUM!

Honey Mustard Pork Tenderloin with Wilted Arugula
Yields: 4 Servings

Ingredients:

12 oz. pork tenderloin
4 oz. prosciutto – sliced
4 cups arugula
½ cup water
¼ cup Dijon mustard
4 tablespoons ghee (clarified butter)
4 tablespoons raw honey
2 tablespoons olive oil
1 tablespoon minced garlic

Method:
1. Heat the olive oil in a non- stick pan over a medium high heat.
2. While the pan heats mix the pork and prosciutto with the honey and mustard taking care to ensure it is all well coated.
3. Place the pork mixture in the pan and cook for 2 – 3 minutes.
4. Remove the pork from the pan and deglaze the pan with water scraping all the yummy bits off the bottom of the pan with a wooden spoon.
5. Now add the ghee to the hot pan along with the garlic and allow it to melt and infuse.
6. Remove the pan from the heat and add the arugula to the pan, tossing it well in the garlic-ghee "sauce".
7. Serve the garlic arugula over the honey mustard pork.
8. A smorgasbord of delightful flavor – enjoy!

Balsamic Pork Tenderloin
Yields: 2 Servings

Ingredients:

1 lb. pork tenderloin fillet – trimmed of all visible fat and sliced into medallions
1 onion – thinly sliced
½ cup balsamic vinegar
2 tablespoons olive oil
2 tablespoons minced garlic

Method:
1. Pour the balsamic over the pork medallions and set aside.
2. Heat up the olive oil in a large non-stick pan over a medium high heat, then add the garlic and onions.
3. Sauté for about 1 minute, then add the pork and cook over a high heat until the pork is cooked through (3 – 4 minutes).
4. Serve with a side of cauliflower rice with the pan juices poured over.
5. Unbelievable taste!

Pork Chops and Apple Sauce
Yields: 2 Servings

Ingredients:

2 thin pork chops
½ cup Paleo apple sauce
¼ cup apple juice – no sugar added
2 tablespoons ghee
2 tablespoons olive oil
Salt and pepper to taste

Method:
1. Heat up the olive oil in a non-stick pan and season the pork chops with a little salt and pepper.
2. Cook over a medium high heat until brown on both sides – about 2 minutes per side.
3. Remove the pork chops from the pan and pour in the apple juice to deglaze and scrape all the caramelized bits off the bottom of the pan with a wooden spoon.
4. Stir in the ghee and pour this rich sauce over the pork chops.
5. Serve them with some Paleo friendly apple sauce on the side.
6. Traditional, hearty food at its best!

Breakneck Beef

Taco's with a Twist
Yields: 1 Serving

<u>*Ingredients:*</u>

¼ lb. ground beef
2 eggs - beaten
1 green chili – seeds removed and chopped
½ an avocado - sliced
2 tablespoons Paleo salsa
2 tablespoons olive oil

<u>*Method:*</u>
1. Heat up 2 non-stick pans over a medium high heat and add one tablespoon of olive oil to each.
2. In one pan, add the ground beef and cook until browned.
3. In the other, add the eggs and cook until brown, then flip it over and cook the other side. This will be your "taco shell".
4. While the food cooks, slice up your avocado and chop your chili.
5. To assemble your taco's, lay the egg on a plate and spread the beef over one half. Top with the green chili and avocado slices and lastly finish off with the salsa.
6. Fold the empty half of the egg over the filling and serve.
7. Yummy and quick!

Minute Steaks with Wilted Spinach
Yields: 4 Servings

Ingredients:

4 sirloin steaks
1 lb. baby spinach leaves
1 red onion – thinly sliced
1 red pepper – julienned
4 garlic cloves - chopped
1 cup organic or homemade beef stock
¼ cup balsamic vinegar
¼ cup olive oil
¼ cup freshly chopped oregano

Method:
1. Heat up 2 tablespoons of olive oil in a non-stick pan over a medium high heat.
2. While the pan heats up, pound the sirloin steaks until they are ½ an inch thick, then place them in the hot pan and sear them on both sides.
3. Remove the steak from the pan and add the rest of the olive oil, the onions, peppers, garlic and sauté for 1 minute, then add the stock, balsamic and oregano.
4. Place the meat back into the pan and add the baby spinach leaves.
5. Allow to cook until they are just beginning to wilt and then serve.
6. Amazing flavor and so simple to prepare!

Pepper Beef Stir Fry
Yields: 4 Servings

Ingredients:

1 lb. beef – cut into strips
¼ cup coconut aminos
1 onion – thinly sliced
1 red pepper – thinly sliced
1 green pepper – thinly sliced
1 yellow pepper – thinly sliced
4 garlic cloves – minced
2 tablespoons sesame oil
1 teaspoon freshly grated ginger

Method:
1. Heat up the sesame oil in a non-stick pan over a high heat and add the garlic, ginger and onions.
2. Cook for 1 minute and then add the beef and coconut aminos.
3. Brown the beef for 2 minutes and then throw in the peppers.
4. Continue to sauté on high until the peppers are tender crisp – about 2 minutes.
5. Serve immediately and devour!

Steak n Egg with Paleo "Fries"
Yields: 2 Servings

Ingredients:

2 sirloin steaks – pounded thin
2 sweet potatoes – washed and blemishes removed
1 red or green pepper – cored and sliced into thick rounds
4 eggs
4 tablespoons olive oil
1 teaspoon paprika
Salt and pepper to taste

Method:
1. Rub the sweet potatoes with 1 tablespoon each of olive oil and season them with salt and pepper.
2. Poke a few holes in them and place them on a microwaveable plate. Cook on high for 5 minutes.
3. While the potatoes cook, heat up the rest of the olive oil in a large non-stick pan over a medium high heat and season the steak with salt and pepper.
4. Place the steak in the middle of the pan, and lay 4 pepper rings around the edge (if your pan isn't big enough, use 2 pans).
5. Crack one egg into the middle of each pepper ring and allow to cook for 5 minutes.
6. Turn the steak over once during the cooking time.
7. Serve and enjoy.
8. This dish is amazing!

Beef Carpaccio
Yields: 2 – 4 Servings

Ingredients:

1 lb. filet mignon – partially frozen
4 cups arugula
Salt and pepper to taste
Olive oil to taste
Lemon juice to taste

Method:
1. 2 Slice the frozen steak paper thin onto a serving plate. You can use a meat slicer if you have it or just a very sharp knife.
2. Lay all the pieces out into a layer that is only just overlapping slightly.
3. Top the steak with the arugula.
4. Drizzle olive oil and lemon juice over the top and season with salt and pepper.
5. Serve and enjoy!

Lickety Split Lamb

Minty Lamb Burgers
Yields: 4 Servings

Ingredients:

1 lb. ground lamb
¼ cup finely chopped mint
1 tablespoon olive oil
Salt and pepper to taste

Method:
1. Heat up the olive oil in a non-stick pan over a medium heat.
2. Mix the ground lamb and mint together well and season with salt and pepper.
3. Form the mixture into 4 equal sized patties and press down so they are not too thick.
4. Fry in the pan until cooked through and brown.
5. Serve with a tossed green salad.
6. Oh so Yummy!!!!

Pepper Crusted Lamb Chops with Fruit Salsa
Yields: 2 – 4 Servings

Ingredients:

4 lamb chops – pounded thin (about 1 inch thick)
2 cups mango – diced
½ cup kiwi fruit - diced
½ cup red onion – finely diced
1 jalapeno – finely diced
4 tablespoons freshly chopped mint
2 tablespoons raw honey
2 tablespoons olive oil
Juice of 1 lime
Black pepper to taste

Method:
1. Heat up the olive oil in a non-stick pan and season the lamb chops generously with black pepper.
2. Fry the chops over a medium high heat for 5 minutes, turning once half way through the cooking time (cook for longer if you prefer more well-done meat).
3. While the chops cook, mix the rest of the ingredients together to make the fruit salsa.
4. Top the cooked chops with the fresh fruity salsa and serve.
5. Deliciously refreshing – enjoy!

Fish in a Flash and Snappy Seafood

Apple-Walnut Tuna Salad
Yields: 2 Servings

Ingredients:

½ lb. canned light tuna
1 apple – cored and chopped
4 cups baby spinach leaves
½ cup Paleo Mayonnaise
¼ cup walnuts – roughly chopped
2 tablespoons finely chopped celery
2 tablespoons dill
2 tablespoons raw honey
½ teaspoon garlic powder
Salt and pepper to taste

Method:
1. Drain the tuna and place it into a big salad bowl.
2. Add the apple, dill, walnuts, celery, honey, garlic powder, salt and pepper and mix well.
3. Serve over a bed of baby spinach leaves with Paleo mayonnaise drizzled over.
4. An absolute explosion of tastes and textures. Enjoy!

Shrimp on the Barbie
Yields: 2 Servings

Ingredients:

1 lb. large shrimp – shelled and deveined
¼ cup almonds - slivered
1 bunch thyme
Zest of 1 lemon
Juice of 1 lemon
4 garlic cloves – chopped
4 tablespoons ghee
Olive oil to brush on the grill
Salt and pepper to taste

Method:
1. Fire up the Gas Grill!
2. Brush with some olive oil.
3. While the grill heats, skewer the shrimp on the thyme stalks and season with salt and pepper.
4. Grill the shrimp until they are pink and cooked through – about 2 minutes per side.
5. While the shrimp cook, prepare your sauce.
6. Melt the ghee in a non-stick pan over a medium high heat.
7. Add the garlic, lemon juice, almonds, and lemon zest. Stir so all the flavors infuse the butter.
8. Pour this delicious sauce over the shrimp and serve with crisp salad greens.
9. Amazing!

Mustard Crusted Tilapia and Coleslaw
Yields: 4 – 6 Servings

Ingredients for the Tilapia:
6 tilapia fillets – about 1 inch thick
1 cup almond flour
½ cup chives – chopped
3 tablespoons Dijon mustard
2 tablespoons olive oil
1 tablespoon garlic powder
Salt and pepper to taste

Ingredients for the Coleslaw:
2 cups shredded white cabbage
2 cups shredded red cabbage
1 cup shredded apple
½ cup walnuts – chopped
4 tablespoons walnut oil
4 tablespoons Paleo mayonnaise
2 tablespoons apple cider vinegar
1 teaspoon Dijon mustard
Salt and pepper to taste

Method:
1. Mix the almond flour with the chives, salt, pepper and garlic powder.
2. Heat up the olive oil in a non-stick pan over a medium high heat.
3. Spread ½ tablespoon Dijon mustard onto each fish fillet and then place them into the seasoned flour mustard side down.
4. Cook the fish in the hot pan for 2 minutes on each side.
5. While the fish cooks, add the apples, walnuts and cabbage to a large mixing bowl. Whisk the rest of the

coleslaw ingredients together, pour over the coleslaw and toss to combine.

6. Serve the fish with a side of coleslaw and enjoy.
7. YUMMY!

Salmon Wraps
Yields: 2 Servings

<u>*Ingredients*</u>:

4 large romaine lettuce leaves
4 oz. smoked salmon
¼ cup red onion – finely diced
¼ cup cucumber – thinly sliced
1 teaspoon lemon zest
½ teaspoon cracked black pepper

<u>*Method*</u>:
1. Lay the lettuce leaves on a plate and sprinkle them with the lemon zest and black pepper.
2. Lay the smoked salmon on top and evenly distribute the onion and cucumber slices.
3. Wrap them up and devour!
4. Totally awesome and ridiculously simple!

Asian-Style Shrimp
Yields: 4 – 6 Servings

Ingredients:

2 lb. shrimp – raw and peeled with the tails still on
¼ cup freshly chopped coriander
6 garlic cloves - minced
4 tablespoons coconut oil
2 tablespoons coconut aminos
2 tablespoons fish sauce
1 tablespoon lemon juice
Salt and black pepper to taste

Method:

1. Melt the coconut oil in a large non-stick pan over a medium high heat and add the garlic.
2. Stir for 1 minute and then add the shrimp.
3. Sauté the shrimp for 2 minutes and then add the rest of the ingredients except the coriander and cook until the shrimp are pink through.
4. Serve the shrimp with the pan juices poured over and a sprinkling of freshly chopped coriander.
5. Quick easy and tasty!

Smoked Salmon Sushi Rolls
Yields: 4 Servings

Ingredients:

4 oz. grated cucumber
2 oz. avocado
2 oz. smoked salmon
2 pieces nori
2 tablespoons red pepper – grated
1 teaspoon lime juice
½ teaspoon grated ginger

Method:
1. Mash the avocado, ginger and lime juice together in a bowl.
2. Lay the nori shiny side down on a clean work surface and spread the avocado mixture in an even layer over the nori.
3. Lay the rest of the ingredients in a band along one side of the nori and then carefully roll it up.
4. Use a very sharp knife to slice the nori roll into equal pieces. Serve with wasabi and coconut aminos.
5. Decadent indulgence!

Gambas
Yields: 2 Servings

Ingredients:

1 lb. shrimp – peeled and deveined
8 garlic cloves - minced
2 tablespoons olive oil
1 tablespoons smoked paprika
1 tablespoon parsley – finely chopped
1 teaspoon red pepper flakes
Juice of 1 lemon
Salt and pepper to taste

Method:

1. Heat up the olive oil in a large non-stick pan over a medium heat and sauté the minced garlic for 1 minute until it starts to brown, then add the paprika and red pepper flakes.
2. Add the shrimp and cook for a minute or two depending on the size and toss well to coat with the garlic.
3. Remove the pan from the heat, squeeze over the lemon juice, sprinkle on the parsley and season with some salt and pepper to taste.
4. Serve immediately with a crisp salad or if you have a little time, mashed root vegetables are an excellent accompaniment to the shrimp.
5. Eat up and enjoy!

Pan Seared Citrus Scallops
Yields: 2 Servings

<u>*Ingredients:*</u>

12 scallops
2 zucchini – top and tailed and cut into 12 rounds of even thickness
½ an onion - minced
3 tablespoons olive oil
2 tablespoons orange juice
2 tablespoons lemon juice
Zest of 1 lemon
Zest and juice of 1 lime
Zest of 1 orange
Salt and black pepper to taste

<u>*Method:*</u>
1. Heat up 2 non-stick pans over a medium high heat and add 1 tablespoon of olive oil to each.
2. Heat up a griddle pan over a medium high heat and add 1 tablespoons of olive oil to it.
3. Place the zucchini rounds into the griddle pan and cook them for 2 minutes per side.
4. Place the onion into the one non-stick pan and cook for 1 minute, then add the scallops and cook for 2 minutes until they are opaque throughout.
5. Lastly add the lemon, lime and orange juice to the pan and give it a stir.
6. While the scallops are cooking, add the zest to the last pan and stir it around to release the citrus flavors.
7. To serve, Place the zucchini rounds onto a serving platter and top each one with a scallop. Lastly sprinkle the citrus zest over the top and serve with a drizzle of olive oil.
8. Absolutely superb!

Cod Sticks
Yields: 1 Serving

Ingredients:

12 oz. cod fillets – cut into 12 strips
½ cup almond flour
2 eggs – beaten
2 tablespoons olive oil
1 teaspoon paprika
Salt and pepper to taste

Method:
1. Season the almond flour with the paprika, salt and pepper.
2. Heat up the olive oil in a non-stick pan over a medium high heat.
3. Dip the cod strips into the beaten eggs and then coat them in the seasoned almond flour.
4. Add them to the hot pan and fry them until they are golden brown on both sides – about 2 minute per side.
5. Serve atop a bed of crisp salad greens with a drizzle of balsamic and olive oil.
6. Totally divine!

Crab Cakes with Homemade Tartar Sauce
Yields: 4 Servings

Ingredients for the Crab Cakes:
12 oz. canned crab meat – drained
1 cup almond flour
½ cup red pepper – finely diced
½ cup onion – finely diced
¼ cup fresh parsley
2 tablespoons fresh dill
2 tablespoons lemon juice
2 tablespoons olive oil
2 eggs

Ingredients for the Tartar Sauce:
¼ cup Paleo mayonnaise
1 dill pickle – finely chopped
2 tablespoons fresh lemon juice
1 tablespoons fresh dill
1 tablespoon chives - chopped
1 teaspoon Dijon mustard
½ teaspoon dried parsley

Method:
1. To make the crab cakes, combine everything except the olive oil in the food processor and blend.
2. While the blender is running, heat up the olive oil in a non-stick pan over a medium heat
3. Form the mixture into 8 even sized balls and flatten them.
4. Place the crab cakes into the pan and cook for 5 minutes, turning once half way through the cooking time.
5. While the crab cakes are cooking, make the tartar sauce.

6. Mix all the ingredients together in a bowl and set aside.
7. Serve the crab cakes on a bed of salad greens with the tartar sauce on the side.
8. Quick, easy and scrumptious – it doesn't get better than this!

Tuna Tataki
Yields: 4 Servings

<u>*Ingredients:*</u>

4 tuna steaks
½ cup sesame oil
¼ cup coconut aminos
1 tablespoons minced garlic
1 tablespoons grated ginger
4 teaspoons black pepper
1 teaspoon of 5 spice powder

<u>*Method:*</u>
1. Heat up a non-stick pan over a high heat.
2. Season the tuna steaks with the black pepper and then sear them in the hot pan.
3. Remove the tuna from the heat and slice it into strips (It will be seared on the outside but still raw on the inside).
4. Whisk the rest of the ingredients together in a bowl and serve as a dipping sauce for the tuna strips.
5. A wonderfully tasty light meal to enjoy!

Seafood Stir Fry
Yields: 4 Servings

Ingredients:

12 scallops
12 shrimp – peeled and deveined
1 green pepper – julienned
1 onion – thinly sliced
4 garlic cloves - minced
4 tablespoons coconut aminos
2 tablespoons olive oil
1 teaspoon cumin
½ teaspoon chili powder
Salt and pepper to taste

Method:
1. Heat up the olive oil in a non-stick pan over a medium high heat and add the garlic and spices.
2. Cook for a minute until the spices become fragrant.
3. Add the onions and green pepper and cook for another minute until they begin to soften, then add the scallops and shrimp.
4. Cook until the seafood is opaque – about 3 minutes.
5. Season with salt and pepper and serve immediately.
6. Simple and tasty!

Sweet and Sour Salmon Fillet
Yields: 1 Serving

Ingredients:

1 salmon fillet
2 tablespoons honey
1 tablespoon coconut aminos
1 tablespoon olive oil
1 teaspoon ground ginger
Salt and pepper to taste

Method:
1. Season the salmon fillet with salt, pepper and the ground ginger.
2. Heat up the olive oil in a non-stick pan and add the salmon.
3. Cook for 2 minutes per side.
4. While the salmon cooks, whisk the honey and coconut aminos together and pour over the salmon just before you remove it from the pan.
5. Serve the salmon with some fresh salad greens.
6. Tuck in and enjoy!

Scallops with Cucumber-Mango Salsa
Yields: 2 Servings

<u>*Ingredients:*</u>

½ lb. scallops
½ cup mango – diced
½ cup cucumber – peeled and chopped
1 tablespoon freshly chopped coriander
1 tablespoon olive oil
1 teaspoon grated ginger
Juice and zest of 1 lime
Salt and pepper to taste

<u>*Method:*</u>
1. Heat up the oil in a non-stick pan over a medium high heat and season the scallops with salt and pepper.
2. Add the scallops to the pan and sear them until they are starting to turn brown – about 2 minutes on each side.
3. While the scallops are cooking, mix the rest of the ingredients together to make a mango salsa.
4. Serve the scallops with the mango salsa on the side.
5. YUMMY!

Conclusion

Thank you again for purchasing this book!

I hope it was able to help you to realize that you can put together a balanced meal with a more well-rounded representation of the food pyramid without expending too much effort or energy. Anyone can make a detour through the drive through or stick some mac and cheese into the microwave, but at what cost?

I certainly think you will agree that your health is not the price we should be paying for the "convenience" of fast food. And with this book in your possession, you will never have to make that choice again.

The next step is to test out these recipes for yourself and perfect your favorites. Happy cooking and most of all happy Paleo eating!

Finally, if you enjoyed this book, please take the time to share your thoughts and post a review on Amazon. It'd be greatly appreciated!

Thank you and good luck!

Lucy Fast

Check out the other Yummy books in my Paleo Diet Solution Series!!

http://www.amazon.com/dp/B00HH1GBLC

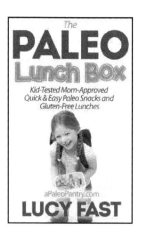

http://www.amazon.com/dp/B00HH1GFRC

http://www.amazon.com/dp/B00HRMZE28

http://www.amazon.com/dp/B00HYKJCZ8

http://www.amazon.com/dp/B00I17R1ZQ

http://www.amazon.com/dp/B00I64CRQW

32235104R00029

Made in the USA
San Bernardino, CA
12 April 2019